Behavior Mapping

A Visual Strategy for Teaching Appropriate Behavior to Individuals With Autism Spectrum and Related Disorders

Amy Buie, MEd, BCBA, LBA

©2013 AAPC Publishing
P.O. Box 23173
Shawnee Mission, Kansas 66283-0173
www.aapcpublishing.net

Publisher's Cataloging-in-Publication

Buie, Amy.

Behavior mapping : a visual strategy for teaching appropriate behavior to individuals with autism spectrum and related disorders / Amy Buie. -- Shawnee Mission, Kan. : AAPC Publishing, c2013.

p. ; cm.
ISBN: 978-1-937473-82-2
LCCN: 2013947203

Includes bibliographical references.
Summary: A manual for creating visual maps to help students whose primary learning style is visual become better problem solvers by literally showing them cause and effect and choices in various situations. The ultimate goal is to make students more successful learners and reduce the incidence of unacceptable behavior.--Publisher.

1. Autistic children--Behavior modification--Study and teaching. 2. Children with autism spectrum disorders--Behavior modification--Study and teaching. 3. Learning disabled children--Behavior modification--Study and teaching. 4. Social skills--Study and teaching. 5. Visual learning. 6. Autistic children--Education. 7. Children with autism spectrum disorders--Education. 8. Learning disabled children--Education. 9. Teachers of children with disabilities--Handbooks, manuals, etc. I. Title.

LC4717.8 .B85 2013
371.94--dc23   1309

This book is designed in Myriad Pro.

Printed in the United States of America.

Interior Art: © thinkstockphotos.com

Acknowledgments

A special thanks to my wonderful teachers and staff, who work hard every day to change the lives of the students in their care. The Center for Autism Education is blessed to have such a wonderful group of professionals. Thanks for all you do!

A big thank-you to Eric Wieringa for helping me draw the Behavior Maps. They look beautiful compared to mine, using my very basic drawing skills.

Also, thank you to Tara Hays for her help in creating my web-based program for making easy-to-use Behavior Maps (www.behaviormapping.com).

Finally, thanks to my family – my husband Brian, and my kids, Alex, Andrew, and Katie. Your patience and love gave me the support to finally bring my dream for this book to reality.

Table of Contents

Introduction

Seeing a growing need for effective programming, in 1998 I opened a classroom for children with autism and other developmental disabilities. Some of my students spent most of their time with me; others spent part of their day with me but most of their time in the general education setting. We worked on math, reading, and social studies as well as various life skills.

We also worked on behavior issues that inevitably occurred throughout the week due to changes in the schedule, difficult assignments, and other challenges. While I had many supports in place, some of the students still struggled with refusals, meltdowns, and tantrums.

I generally used visual supports such as social narratives (e.g., Gray, 2010), cartooning (e.g., Gray, 1994), visual schedules, and structured teaching (TEACCH; Schopler, Mesibov, & Hearsey, 1995), which significantly helped each one of the students. However, as I observed and worked with the students with autism spectrum disorders (ASD), I discovered something that changed my classroom dramatically.

One day, it suddenly occurred to me that when it came to redirecting behavior, I was TELLING the students what to do instead of SHOWING them what to do using a visual support. Every day, I SHOWED them their schedule using words and pictures, and I SHOWED them what to do if the schedule changed with a social narrative. However, if I wanted to let them know that good behavior would earn them time with a toy or reinforcer or that inappropriate behavior would mean they did not get time with the toy or other reinforcer, I just TOLD them with words. When my students started getting off track by using a loud voice, for example, I would just say, "Remember, you are working for movie time. Let's use a quiet voice."

In other words, I realized that I was not using visual supports, which are often so effective for children and adults with ASD. That's when I developed a strategy I called Behavior Mapping. Behavior Mapping is a visual strategy that helps children make good choices with regard to their behavior by visually SHOWING them the consequences for each action they choose at any given time.

Visual Supports and Children With ASD

Children with ASD benefit from visual strategies to do well both in school and at home (MacDuff, Krantz, & McClannahan, 1993). For example, social narratives, including Social Stories™ (Gray, 2010), and cartooning, including Comic Strip Conversations™ (Gray, 1994), as well as visual supports like picture schedules have long proven to be effective.

In addition, the Incredible 5-Point Scale (Buron & Curtis, 2012) is an essential tool to assist children with their behavior. Used for a variety of purposes, the 5-Point Scale gives children a visual scale with which to rate how they are feeling and help them see what social behaviors are appropriate for a given level. For example, a "5" might be explained as feeling extremely angry and explosive, whereas a "3" would signify frustrated and a "1" would mean just a little annoyed. By assigning numbers like this, the strategy helps children to communicate how they are feeling, which in turn enables adults and other caregivers to assist them with the choices they can make when those feelings arise.

Another effective visual strategy, Social Behavior Mapping® (Winner, 2007), presents what happens from a social standpoint when children choose certain behaviors, specifically not only how a given choice makes the child feel but also how others feel about the child. For example, Social Behavior Mapping® can be used to show a child that "raising her hand" will help (a) the teacher know she is participating in class, (b) her peers to see she is engaged and paying attention, and (c) the child herself to feel proud and happy. Also part of Winner's Social Behavior Mapping® is the Social Behavior Map®, which shows the child how people feel or react when she behaves in a way that might be considered the "wrong choice."

Behavior Mapping

Behavior Mapping, the focus of this book, complements other visual strategies that are available to support children with ASD, but it is different in two primary ways.

First, Behavior Maps list the reinforcement that will occur for each behavior choice. For example, if the target behavior is to raise one's hand to get the teacher's attention in class rather than blurting out, the Behavior Map indicates the reinforcer for doing so, such as a sticker on the student's sticker chart or time to play with a Buzz Light Year figure, specifically chosen by the child. The Behavior Map also indicates what the consequence would be if the child "shouts out" and does NOT raise his hand; in this case, NO time with Buzz Light Year. As such, Behavior Maps visually show kids how they can earn the things they like by doing what teachers and parents want them to do.

Second, Behavior Maps are created by teachers and caregivers who determine and specify ahead of time what the consequences of a given behavior will be. That is, the creator of the Behavior Map has control over the consequence that the child will experience when a given behavior occurs. For example, using the example above, based on a reinforcement menu for the individual child, the teacher identified that the child liked Buzz Light Year and then created a map to teach a new behavior such as "raise your hand." The adult chooses the consequence for the child and the Behavior Map visually shows this to the child.

Over the last 15 years, I have utilized and perfected Behavior Mapping in my classroom with students with very severe and challenging behaviors at the Center for Autism Education in O'Fallon, Missouri. Combined with other supports such as those mentioned above, I have found it to be one of the most effective strategies to reduce problem behavior for children who have ASD and related disabilities.

As I prepared to publish this book, I reviewed the research to see if others were using a similar strategy and having any success. I was thrilled to find that maps were used with success with a child with autism in Canada. I created Behavior Mapping for my classroom in 1998. In 2004, a student at the University of British Columbia discovered the same thing I had discovered: Behavior Maps are very effective for children with autism and related disorders. Brown later published an article on his use of the strategy, which he called contingency mapping (Brown & Mirenda, 2006).

Later a study was conducted by Catherine Tobin and Richard Simpson (2012), based on the work of Brown and Mirenda (2006), on the use of Consequence Maps with a 6-year-old student with a primary diagnosis of emotional disturbance, ADHD, and oppositional defiant disorder. Results of the study indicated that the Consequence Maps used in the study reduced some of the child's non-compliant behavior, which included refusing and some aggression. This early research further supports the use of mapping for children who demonstrate significant behavior.

In addition, the Lee's Summit School District in Missouri is using Consequence Maps with their students. The book *How to Reach and Teach Children with Challenging Behavior – Practical, Ready-to-Use Interventions That Work* by Kaye Otten and Jodie Tuttle (2011) shows some examples of how they have been using the maps. A variation on the Consequence Map includes a map that says, "What might happen if" at the top. This is a great way to help students start creating their own maps when they are ready.

Why Use Behavior Maps?

In working with children with ASD, I have learned that many do not understand the concept of cause and effect. That is, when behaviors lead to consequences, students are often unaware of how their actions resulted in those consequences. In addition, even higher functioning children who have language skills typically do not have the language to negotiate, ask for clarification, or repair language during conversations with others – pragmatic language. For example, when we are in conversation with others and the person we are talking to has a "I don't understand you" look on his face, we "repair" our language by explaining things in another way and asking questions to clarify and/or confirm understanding.

Not only are cause and effect as well as pragmatic language difficult for children with ASD, these children tend to be very rigid and even compulsive about the events in their lives (Myles & Southwick, 2005), which leads to "rigid thinking," or difficulty seeing things in more than one way. Indeed, one of the characteristics of autism includes a restricted range of activities (American Psychiatric Association, 2013). This can be seen in the way children play with toys (perhaps lining up a toy over and over instead of using it in pretend play) or in an intense preoccupation or obsession (such as fans or vacuum cleaners). This restricted range of interests and activities includes challenges relating to objects and events. Thus, children with ASD want things to go a certain way and have great difficulty when things change. At times, their frustration over not being able to process and accept change leads to behavior problems (Volkmar, Klin, & Cohen,1997), such as refusing to work or hitting and kicking.

This is where Behavior Maps come in. A Behavior Map helps children understand cause and effect, specifically how their behavior (cause) leads to consequences (effect). Behavior Maps also allow children to see (with words and pictures) how positive choices will lead to rewards, motivating them to make good choices and learn new skills.

Best of all, Behavior Maps are grounded in evidence-based practice as illustrated in the following chart based on the National Autism Center (www.nationalautismcenter.org).

Evidence-Based Practices From the National Autism Center
Correlated With
Behavior Mapping – A Visual Strategy for Teaching Appropriate Behavior to Individuals With Autism Spectrum and Related Disorders

Strategy	Corresponding NAC EBP	Benefits Shown Through Research
CHOICE MAKING*	**ANTECEDENT PACKAGE** (changes in the environment before a problematic behavior occurs)	Communication skills, interpersonal (or social) skills, personal responsibility, play skills, self-regulation, sensory and emotional regulation
TEACHING ALTERNATIVE SKILLS	**BEHAVIORAL PACKAGE** (changes in the environment before and after a problematic behavior occurs)	Communication skills, interpersonal (or social) skills, personal responsibility, play skills, self-regulation, restricted, repetitive, nonfunctional patterns of behavior, sensory and emotional regulation and reduction of problem behavior
POSITIVE REINFORCEMENT	**BEHAVIORAL PACKAGE** (changes in the environment before and after a problematic behavior occurs)	Communication skills, interpersonal (or social) skills, personal responsibility, play skills, self-regulation, restricted, repetitive, nonfunctional patterns of behavior, sensory and emotional regulation and reduction of problem behaviors
MODELING	**MODELING** (Adults or peers demonstrate a target behavior so it is imitated by the individual)	Communication skills, higher cognitive functions, interpersonal (or social) skills, play skills, and self-regulation
DIFFERENTIAL REINFORCEMENT	**BEHAVIORAL PACKAGE** (changes in the environment before and after a problematic behavior occurs)	Communication skills, interpersonal (or social) skills, personal responsibility, play skills, self-regulation, restricted, repetitive, nonfunctional patterns of behavior, sensory and emotional regulation and reduction of problem behaviors
SOCIAL NARRATIVES	**STORY-BASED INTERVENTION PACKAGE** (written description of the situation under which specific behaviors are expected to occur)	Interpersonal (or social) skills and self-regulation
SELF-MONITORING	**SELF-MANAGEMENT** (teaching individuals to regulate their own behavior)	Interpersonal (or social) skills and self-regulation
PROMPTING*	**ANTECEDENT PACKAGE** (changes in the environment before a problematic behavior occurs)	Communication skills, interpersonal (or social) skills, personal responsibility, play skills, self-regulation, sensory and emotional regulation
SOCIAL SCRIPTS	**STORY-BASED INTERVENTION PACKAGE** (written description of the situation under which specific behaviors are expected to occur)	Interpersonal (or social) skills and self-regulation
SPECIAL INTERESTS	**ANTECEDENT PACKAGE** (changes in the environment before a problematic behavior occurs)	Communication skills, interpersonal (or social) skills, personal responsibility, play skills, self-regulation, restricted, repetitive, nonfunctional patterns of behavior, sensory and emotional regulation and reduction of problem behavior
VISUAL SUPPORTS	**SCHEDULES** (presentation of a task list that communicates a series of activities or steps)	Self-regulation

*Also behavioral package.

Getting Ready to Use Behavior Mapping

Before implementing this strategy, it is important to make sure that the "basics" are in place.

First, a functional behavior assessment (FBA) with ongoing data collection and evaluation is crucial to every program developed for a child with ASD. As part of an FBA (O'Neill et al., 1997), the team determines the function of the behavior of concern. In other words, what is the child telling you through behaviors such as screaming? It might be, "I want to spend time with you" or "This is hard and I don't want to do it."

Second, children need a visual and premacked schedule (preferred activity after every non-preferred activity) that shows them the expectations and plans for each day. Such a schedule can be made using words, pictures, or objects, depending on the level of the student.

Schedules help to predict what is coming next and can help children with ASD understand changes. For example, if outdoor recess is canceled due to weather, a visual picture can "show" the change by removing the picture or crossing off the word "outdoor recess" and replacing it with a picture of the classroom or a word that indicates they will be spending recess inside.

Third, in order to teach appropriate social responses throughout the day, the use of social narratives is essential in planning for a child with ASD. Social narratives can be used to predict upcoming changes. For example, a social narrative could be written to help a child understand a fire drill and the appropriate way to behave (line up quietly, walk outside, wait for the "all clear" to go back to class, etc.). Social narratives should be shared and utilized on a daily basis.

Finally, it is important to provide support for the various sensory challenges that children with ASD encounter. Incoming sensory input that most of us pay little or no attention to, such as lights, noises in the room, smells, and the texture of clothes, can so overwhelm a child that it becomes difficult for him to pay attention, process information, and stay organized in the classroom. This can also cause challenging behaviors. To remedy such situations, it can help to implement sensory breaks in the student's school day, including 5-Point Scales (see page 25) to determine level of stress, and visual supports to request a break, to include time to jump on a trampoline, swing, or relax in a beanbag (Endow, 2011).

When working with students with ASD, or any child, for that matter, any *one* strategy should not be used exclusively. Many children with ASD have trouble with generalization, which involves learning a skill and then performing it with different people, different materials, and different places. As a result, an approach that uses multiple strategies is most effective (Heflin & Alaimo, 2007).

After a general discussion of behavior, the following chapters contain the information you need to design and use four types of Behavior Maps: Consequence Maps, Complex Behavior Maps, Language Maps, and Problem-Solving Maps. To be effective, maps should be individualized for each student. Maps do not need to be presented in a particular order. Choose the type that works for your student based on need. I typically write a map concerning a specific situation, often right when the target behavior occurs.

Maps can help a student understand expectations and calm down, especially if a potential problem is caught early. For the most part, Behavior Maps are used to prevent problem behavior and help kids make good choices. Sometimes, if we can present a Behavior Map to a child early enough during a frustrating situation, we can help him "calm down" and prevent a meltdown.

> As an owner of this book, you may download blank copies of the three major types of Behavior Maps discussed in this book, Consequence Maps, Language Maps, and Problem-Solving Maps, from www.aapcpublishing.net/9107

Chapter 1: Understanding Behavior

The goal of our work with students with ASD is to enable them to participate successfully in school and the community and, therefore, lead meaningful lives as contributing members of society. A major component of this involves supporting them in learning and demonstrating behaviors that are appropriate in a given setting at a given time. We want students to be ready to learn and participate in the classroom without hitting and screaming or be able to go out to dinner without a major tantrum. These goals are usually our top priority. Inappropriate behavior limits children and adults from participating fully in the community and also affects their ability to make friends, hold a job, and so on.

Kiana, a 14 year-old girl with a diagnosis of ASD, first attended the Center for Autism Education about eight years ago. At school, she often screamed, refused to work, hit others, and used profanity. Due to these behaviors, her family was very limited in terms of what activities they could involve their daughter in. For example, it is not easy to go grocery shopping with your daughter or out to dinner if she is constantly yelling, "Shut the hell up …" and otherwise engages in disruptive behaviors.

After intensive intervention and the use of Behavior Maps, Kiana is now able to follow directions with very little yelling and uses "nice words." In addition, her general behavior has improved to a point where her parents can leave her with a respite provider. In fact, when Kiana's parents were able to go out socially for the first time, her dad told me that he and his wife had not gone out to dinner together for eight years as they had not been able to leave Kiana with a respite provider or bring her with them to a restaurant.

But to change behavior, we must first figure out the function of a given behavior. In other words, what is the behavior trying to communicate? Even if not always clear at first, behaviors communicate messages and are in some way "working" for the child. For example, a child who is hitting might be trying to say, "I don't want to do this," "I want to talk to you," or "I'm hungry and want a snack." The hitting behavior "works" for her when parents and teachers respond to the behavior by talking to her during the hitting or giving her a snack.

Sometimes, the behavior "works" by making work and demands go away. This happens when a child hits after being told to do math and is then sent to the principal's office. That is, hitting "worked" to make the math go away.

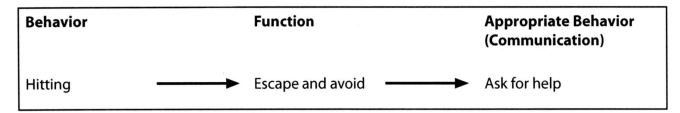

Both children and adults use behavior to communicate due to ineffective communication skills and an inability to regulate their emotion and/or handle changes. Some individuals with ASD do not use verbal language to communicate. If they are on the more severe or classic end of the spectrum, they may have little to no language and also have difficulty processing information due to cognitive and sensory deficits. For example, a student might scream, yell, hit, kick, head-butt, or throw and break things as a way to say "no," ask for help, or request a toy. We want to teach these children to use words, signs, or pictures to tell us what they want or need. As an educator or parent, it is our job to teach children how to communicate in an appropriate way.

Below is a brief example of the results of a functional behavior assessment (FBA). As illustrated, the behavior is "hitting" and the function, as determined by the FBA, is to escape or avoid. Based on the function, the appropriate behavior would be to ask for help verbally (communication).

Behavior	Function	Appropriate Behavior (Communication)
Hitting ⟶	Escape and avoid ⟶	Ask for help

After determining the "function" of a behavior, the next step is to find a behavior that meets the same function but in a more acceptable way. If the child uses behavior such as pinching and screaming to say, "No, I don't want to do what you just asked me to do," we want to teach her a different way to convey the same message. For example, teaching her to say, "This is too hard for me," "I don't feel well," or "I need a break, please" by using sign language or pointing to pictures, will help her learn to use words, signs, or pictures to communicate instead of pinching and screaming. That is, these statements teach her language that meets the same function of escape and avoidance but in a way that is more appropriate and, therefore, more effective.

After determining the function and deciding on a replacement behavior that meets the same function, the next step is to incorporate the strategy into a behavior plan. It is important to write a plan so that everyone knows how to teach the "new" behavior. **Many times when we are ready to write a plan, we forget this first step.** We want to jump in immediately and determine what to do about a behavior before we think about the FBA. We want to know what to do **after** the behavior has occurred so the child learns that it was inappropriate and won't do it again. We often think about things such as timeout or losing a privilege. We might ask, "Should we take recess away or have the student sit in the hallway for a while?" or "Should they lose computer time or go to the principal's office?" After all, something has to be done; he just hit me in the face, and now my nose is bleeding.

These consequences are very typical responses to challenging behavior. We as teachers and caregivers want to do our best to teach the child that some behaviors are not OK. However, a more relevant and effective question than "What do I do about the behavior?" is, "What do you want them to do instead?" This line of thinking takes us away from focusing on giving consequences and leads us to what is needed the most – teaching the child a skill that meets the same function as the behavior we want to change. All of our time and energy needs to be focused on teaching behaviors, not punishing behaviors, as illustrated in the following.

Carlos, a 9-year-old boy with ASD, loved the computer. If he was playing a game and someone came up to stand next to him, he would hit them in the stomach. For years, the team had addressed this behavior by taking the computer away from him. That is, they asked the question, "What should we do about this behavior?" and the answer was to give Carlos a consequence – taking away his computer privilege.

When I started working with Carlos, my first question was, "What do I want him to do instead?" The answer was that I wanted him to ask me to move away if I walked up to him while he was on the computer. Carlos could read, so I wrote on a card, "Move away, Mrs. Buie." I explained to Carlos that he needed to use his words if he wanted to work on the computer by himself and showed him the card. Then, the next time he had free time, I went over and stood by him while he was on the computer. As soon as he attempted to hit, I put the card in front of him. He looked at the card and read the words out loud, "Move away, Mrs. Buie," whereupon I promptly moved away.

By replacing the behavior instead of punishing it, we made progress in a remarkably short amount of time, eliminating the behavior of hitting in a matter of two sessions.

Sometimes consequences are needed, such as when safety is a concern. But when using a consequence, you need to ask yourself: "Will my child/student learn from the consequence?" In other words, if timeout is used for hitting and we want the child to stop hitting, then each time he hits, he has to go sit in a chair for 5 minutes. But would timeout actually prevent the child from hitting the next time? That is, the next time he felt like hitting, would he stop and think, "I'd better not hit because if I hit, I will have to sit in timeout, so I'm going to choose not to hit this time"?

The answer is, "probably not." Many children with ASD and other developmental and emotional disabilities are not able to understand this cause-effect relationship. As a result, when the same situation arises, the child often still hits because he has no other way to communicate the intended message as we have not taught him what we want him to "do instead."

Thinking about the possible consequence does not matter to the child because all he wants is to tell someone, "This is too hard" and that, therefore, he doesn't want to do it. Further, given a history of receiving consequences, the child thinks, "Many times when I hit and kick you, I have a consequence. Sometimes this consequence means I don't have to do the work you just gave me." In this example, the consequence of timeout is actually reinforcing the hitting, making it more likely to be used again instead of stopping the behavior as it was intended.

As mentioned earlier, consequences can be appropriate for other reasons when helping children who have challenging behavior. For example, my son, who has bipolar disorder, goes to his room for timeout when he is aggressive. However, I know that this is an important consequence for him as it enables him to calm down and sends a message to my other children that aggressive behavior is not acceptable. I am consistent with this consequence, and it is necessary for my son (it helps him calm down). I just have to understand that I am not using the consequence to change behavior. I am doing it for other reasons.

Consequences are also important if they are "natural." For example, if you break the computer, you cannot use it any more, or if you don't eat your dinner, you will be hungry later on. These are not consequences that are applied like a timeout or removal of a toy (punishment). They are what occur naturally because of the choices we make.

Learning how to make choices based on consequences is an essential life skill. This is where Behavior Mapping comes in. It teaches kids how to choose behaviors that meet the same function as the original inappropriate behavior (what we want them to "do instead") and shows them how inappropriate behaviors lead to natural consequences.

Behavior Maps are created by the teacher or parent to visually (in words and/or pictures) show children what happens when they make the choices they do. For example, Carlo's Behavior Map might show that if he hits, the teacher will not walk away, and if he gets mad and breaks the computer, the computer will not be available. The Behavior Map would also show that if he uses his words to say, "Move away," the teacher would move away and Carlos would get to stay on the computer. Each day, prior to Carlos going to the computer, the teacher would review the map with him and would continue to do so until he understood and used the new behavior independently. As illustrated above, sometimes this only takes a few tries.

Chapter 2: Consequence Maps

I refer to the first type of Behavior Mapping as basic mapping, or Consequence Maps. With basic mapping, the teacher or parent "maps" out the choices that the child has; for example, when given an assignment or when a request is made to which the child has to respond in some way. Specifically, when presented with morning work, the child is expected to complete the work. Or when the timer goes off, the child is expected to stop an activity and go on to the next activity listed on the visual schedule.

When students make the correct response, they need to be reinforced so they will use the correct behavior again. They need to realize that if they make an appropriate choice, such as finish the work or transition from preferred activities, good things will happen. Consequence Maps allow them to visually "see" what will happen.

To start, simply write the request or expectation inside a circle or bubble (see page 16). Then, draw arrows to other bubbles indicating choices that the child can make. For example, when presented with morning work, the student has the choice to complete the work or sit at her desk and refuse to work.

In reality, there are many more choices in response to being assigned morning work, but limiting the choices to two – (a) what the student frequently does and (b) what you want him to do – helps to simplify the strategy. (In Chapter 3, Behavior Maps that include more choices will be presented.)

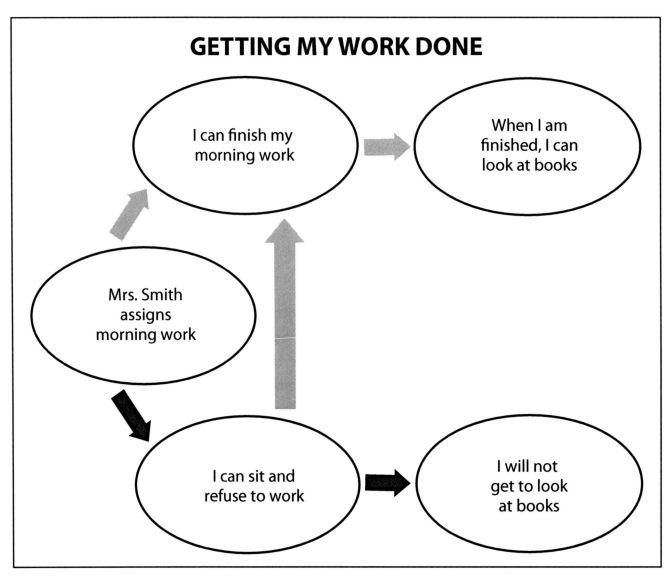

GETTING MY WORK DONE

I can finish my morning work

When I am finished, I can look at books

Mrs. Smith assigns morning work

I can sit and refuse to work

I will not get to look at books

Next, draw arrows that lead to other bubbles to indicate what will happen next. For example, if the child does her morning work, the next bubble might say, "After my work is complete, I can go sit in a bean bag and look at books." If the student chooses not to work, on the other hand, the bubble might say," If I refuse to do my morning work, I will not get to look at books."

I use green arrows to indicate a choice that will lead to a positive outcome, or a "green light" choice, and red arrows to indicate that the choice leads to a natural consequence, or a "red light" choice. In the Behavior Maps in this book, the green arrows are drawn with a gray line and the red arrows are drawn with a solid black line.

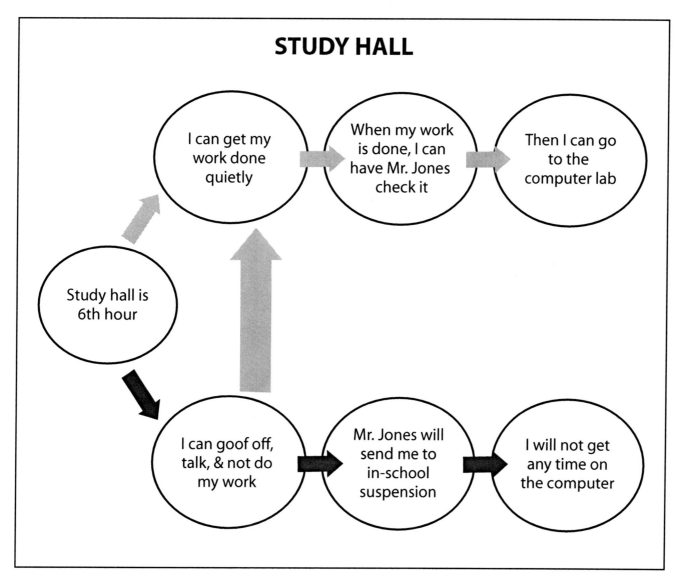

The top of the map always indicates the choice that leads to positive outcomes, along with the reinforcement that will occur after making this choice. In "Getting My Work Done," the student gets to look at books after completing her work. In "Study Hall," the student gets to go to the computer lab after asking the teacher to check her work. In other words, the map gives examples of "what you want the child to do" and shows that by doing so, the child will receive positive reinforcement.

Another important element of a Consequence Map is an arrow to help the child see how she can get reinforcement even if she makes a red light choice initially. That is, most maps should include a green arrow (gray here) to help children see that they can still make the appropriate choice and get "back on track." This does not mean allowing the child to get the reinforcer that she wants after demonstrating an inappropriate behavior. For example, if the child hits, she should not get to look at books. We want her to raise her hand when needing help, so the choice of "raising hand" leads to looking at books, whereas hitting leads to no books.

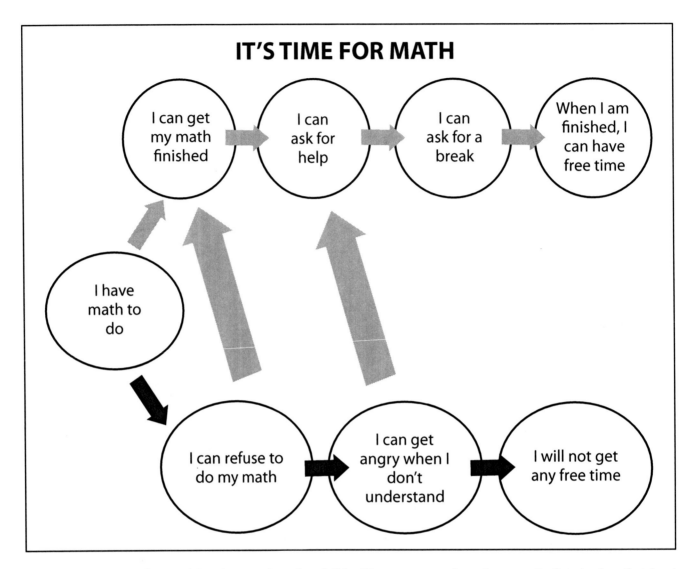

The map "It's Time for Math" indicates that the child will not get any free time until **after** he has finished his math assignment. It does not indicate that free time is taken away; instead, it is contingent upon completing the assigned work. This is an important distinction. If the student chooses not to complete the math, he does **not** get any free time. Giving free time would reinforce the idea that refusing to work would still result in desired activities.

Look carefully at this map again and note that if the student initially chooses not to work, there is a gray arrow (would be green) pointing back to the first bubble that says, "I can get my math sheet finished." Then after the child completes the math sheet, even if it is an hour later, she can have the free time. In other words, it is possible to get back on track toward a positive outcome (and a reinforcer!) even after initially making a "red light" choice.

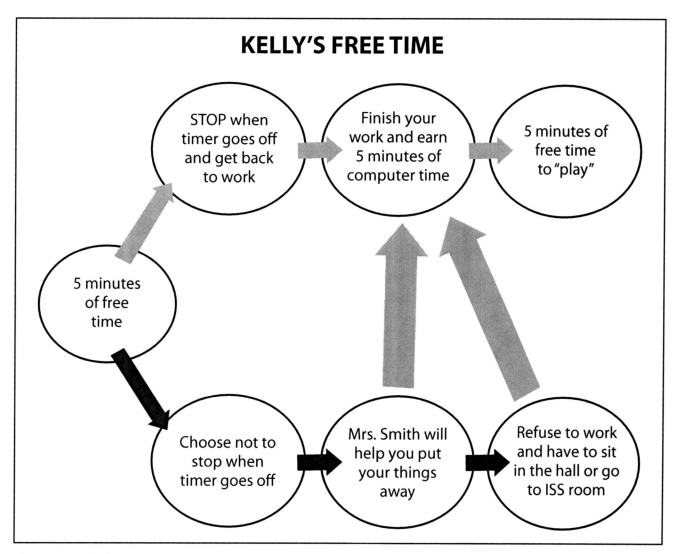

KELLY'S FREE TIME

STOP when timer goes off and get back to work

Finish your work and earn 5 minutes of computer time

5 minutes of free time to "play"

5 minutes of free time

Choose not to stop when timer goes off

Mrs. Smith will help you put your things away

Refuse to work and have to sit in the hall or go to ISS room

The map called "Kelly's Free Time" indicates that Kelly has the choice to stop free-time activities on her own (by stopping when the timer goes off) or leave it up to Mrs. Smith, her teacher, to stop her (by putting Kelly's free-time things away for her). This map does not have a gray/green arrow pointing back to the first bubble. Kelly either makes the right choice or does not. If she chooses not to stop the activity when the timer goes off, you would not want to allow any of her behaviors such as screaming or hitting to get her more free time. More free time would reinforce and teach Kelly that behaviors (such as screaming or hitting) are a way to communicate or ask for the things that she wants (more free time).

If Kelly does not stop and the teacher has to "help" her stop, the teacher would simply step back and allow Kelly to have her tantrum. At that time, it is important NOT to talk to the student. Simply make the environment safe and wait until she is calm again. This might take a while, but it is an important step. Not paying attention to the problem behavior and keeping the student safe will allow her to make a connection to the natural consequence on the Consequence Map.

When we try to prevent tantrums by "giving in" or allowing the child to get what she wants, we prolong the behavior. When Kelly is calm, show her the same map along with her schedule, letting her know your expectations for work completion and your expectations for getting free time again. Never give second chances, but ALWAYS gives second opportunities to try again! A second chance would be letting a child have what he wants AFTER the behavior already occurred. A second opportunity would be to let the child "try again" at a later time so he can be successful.

The Consequence Map called "I Can Have a Good Day" was developed for one of my former students. He often became frustrated and angry throughout the school day. When this happened, he went to a "quiet room" and refused to comply with any request for the rest of the school day. His quiet room was a small room by the counselor's office where he could go to regroup or relax. It was also used if he became unsafe to himself or others by being aggressive.

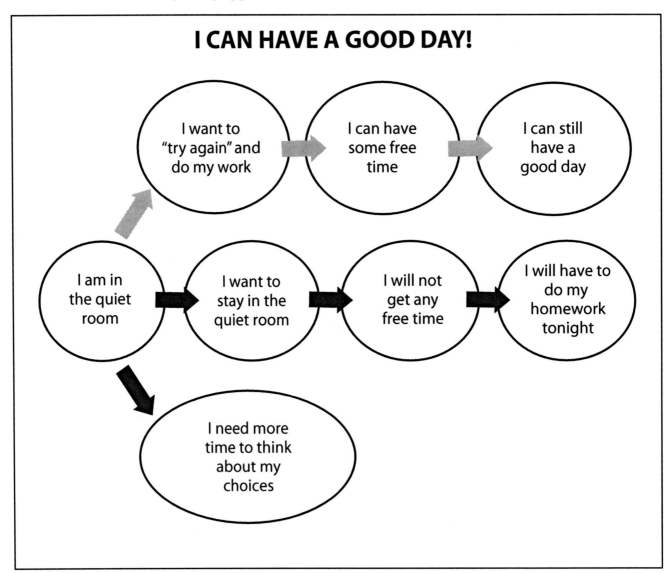

I CAN HAVE A GOOD DAY!

I want to "try again" and do my work → I can have some free time → I can still have a good day

I am in the quiet room → I want to stay in the quiet room → I will not get any free time → I will have to do my homework tonight

I need more time to think about my choices

Once he had an incident, he lacked the language to "negotiate" a way out and, as a result, had a bad day from that point on. As a way to help him get back on track and continue with the rest of the day, I used mapping. It helped him see that he still had choices and the whole day was not "shot."

Many children with ASD need a lot of "think" time, or time to reorganize. It is important not to push them into making a choice before they are ready. Therefore, I added another bubble for this student to choose from saying, "I need more time to think about it." The way this worked was that I sat with the other staff just outside the quiet room, and about every 5-10 minutes I went in and handed him the map. This was nonthreatening to him. He was also allowed to point to his choice instead of coming up with language, which was difficult for him when frustrated or angry.

The final Consequence Maps in this chapter use pictures (picture maps) for non-readers and lower functioning students. These maps make it possible to use the same strategy with students who need even more visual support. In "Andrew Makes Copies," I was able to show a student that when he refrained from hitting, he got to make a copy at the copy machine, which was very reinforcing to him.

ANDREW MAKES COPIES

YES — Andrew works → NO hitting → Andrew makes copies!

NO — No work → Andrew hits → NO copies, Andrew!

The map "Andrew's Marker Time" helped the same student to hold on to a marker as a reinforcer (he earned holding a marker after he got his school work done) for not putting the top in his mouth. I wanted him to have the marker because he worked hard for it. However, I wanted him to see the consequence of not using it safely by putting the top in his mouth. This map allowed Andrew to still earn the marker but use it appropriately.

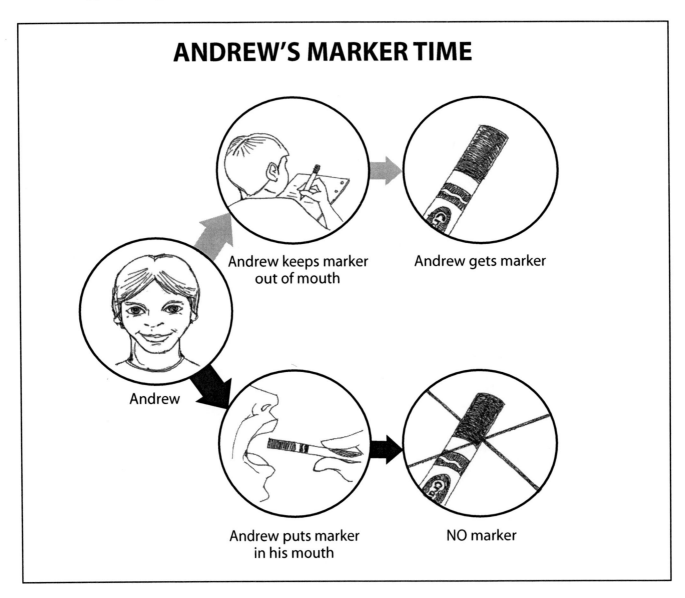

ANDREW'S MARKER TIME

Andrew keeps marker out of mouth

Andrew gets marker

Andrew

Andrew puts marker in his mouth

NO marker

"Using a Quiet Voice" helped one of my students learn to speak quietly, especially when he was frustrated. With this Consequence Map, he was able to see that using a quiet voice, even when frustrated, would get him computer time, time to watch a movie, or time in the swing.

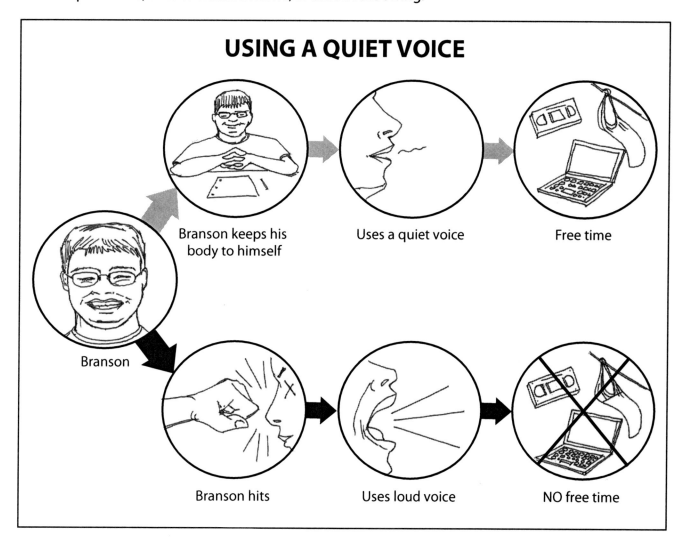

USING A QUIET VOICE

Branson

Branson keeps his body to himself

Uses a quiet voice

Free time

Branson hits

Uses loud voice

NO free time

The final example of a Consequence Map using pictures is "Laurent's Good Choices." I wanted Laurent to use some coping strategies when he got mad, such as asking to jump on the trampoline. As a result of using this map, he made a lot of progress towards using coping skills independently.

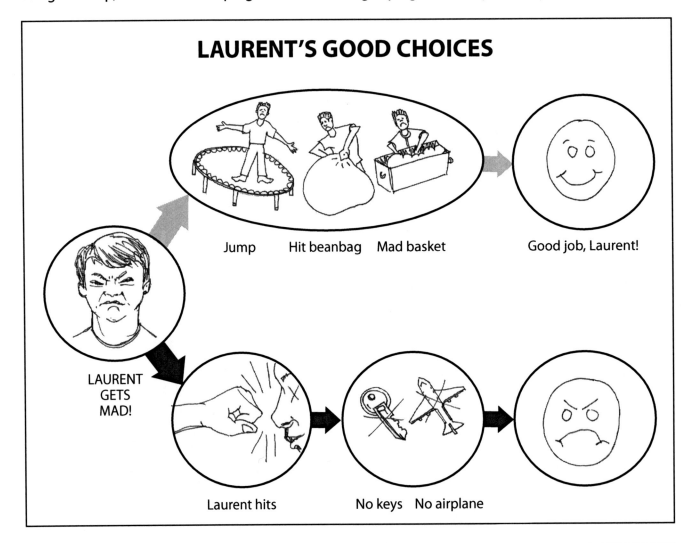

It's important to note that you do not have to be an artist to make a behavior map. Simple hand drawings work fine. If you have trouble drawing, you can use pictures from the Internet or Boardmaker®, a program that makes great pictures for schedules and Consequence Maps (www.mayer-johnson.com/boardmaker). You can also make Behavior Maps with my web-based program (www.behaviormappingmaker.com).

Maps like these allow you to use the same strategy with students of all ages and abilities. In fact, I use many of the examples using pictures for students as young as 3 years old.

Chapter 3: Complex Behavior Mapping

At times, you may want to create more complex maps to provide numerous choices. Remember that the basic Consequence Map gives two choices most of the time to make it concise and simple. Some children may be ready for more choices when presented with a request to complete an assignment or when encountering a situation that causes frustration. In addition, some children advance to more complex Behavior Mapping as they learn to understand cause and effect better.

"When I Feel Angry" was used with a student who often got angry and then started yelling and breaking things, clearly not positive choices. It was important to teach this student about his emotions and to do so in a way that did not suggest they were bad. Through visual prediction in the form of a written scenario, I taught this child that anger is a normal and acceptable feeling and that the important part of learning about feelings is how you deal with them. I wanted him to know that it was OK to be frustrated and upset about things that happened during the day, but that hitting or breaking things was not a good way to express anger and frustration. I wanted to help him see that he could respond to his emotions in other ways, like ask for sensory time, take deep breaths, or ask to take a break. He often calmed down if he could have sensory time to swing or play with a therapy ball, so I wanted to teach him to ask for these things when he was mad. I also used *The Incredible Five-Point Scale* (Buron & Curtis 2012) to assist him in "rating" his level of anger using a scale where 5 meant "really angry" and 1, "a little bit annoyed." Using the map, I showed him what he could do when he rated his anger at a 4 or 5.

From K. D. Buron & M. Curtis. *The Incredible 5-Point Scale: The Significantly Approved and Expanded Second Edition*, 2012. Shawnee Mission, KS: AAPC Publishing. Used with permission.

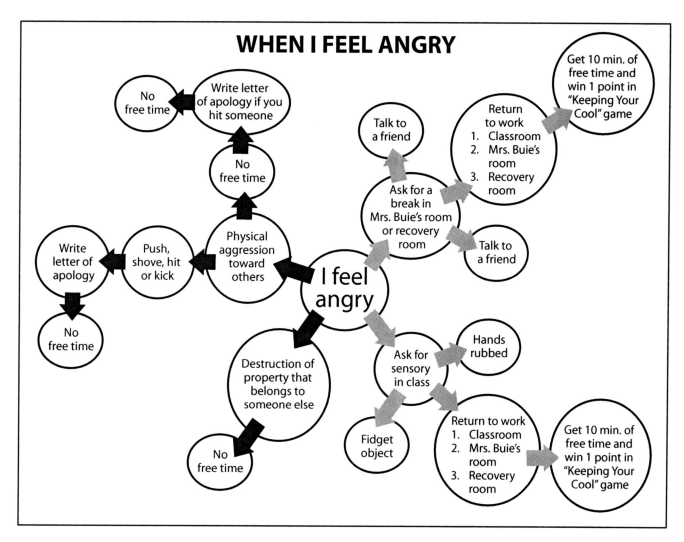

I presented the Complex Map "When I Feel Angry" to the student throughout the school day and in each of his general education classes to teach him both the consequences of taking his anger out on people or property and the alternative choices to make instead that would lead to positive outcomes. In other words, he could ask for sensory time or request a break and get reinforcement for making those green light choices instead of the red light choice of hitting.

With children with ASD, it is important to teach alternative skills through direct instruction and reinforce attempts to use the new skills. If you want a child to ask to take a break, for example, you have to teach her how to do that. Do you want her to raise her hand and say "break," sign "break," hold up a "break card," or point to a picture of "break"?

In addition to directly teaching new skills and behaviors, sometimes including role-playing with peers, it is important to set up a system of reinforcement. For example, offer the student a toy or give a high-five when he demonstrates the desired alternative so he learns to do it again and comes to recognize that following directives and making good choices leads to positive outcomes.

"Will's Choices" uses a different format. The student for whom this Complex Behavior Map was developed engaged in behaviors such as property destruction, screaming/profanity, and aggression when he was bored or angry – behaviors that were inappropriate and very disruptive in the general education classroom. In addition, the attempts from the paraprofessional to redirect him by telling him to stop or use a quiet voice were also disruptive.

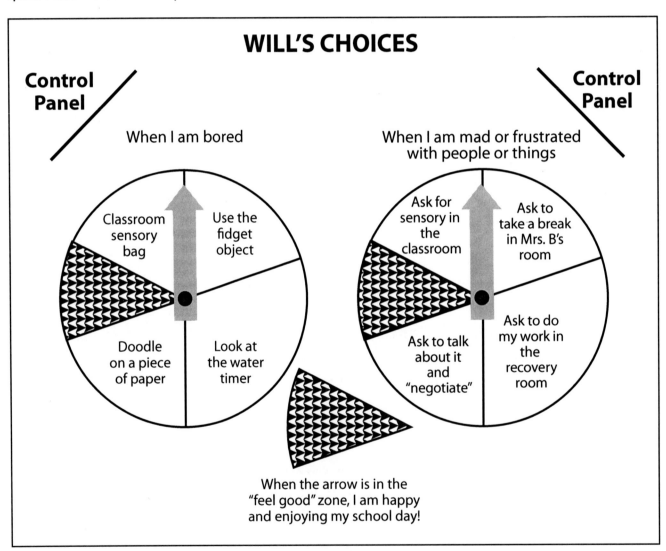

This visual support capitalized on the student's love of aircraft carriers and fighter planes, using the format of a "control panel" to reinforce the idea that he needed to keep his behaviors in "control" just like an airplane needs to stay in "control." The map was placed on Will's desk right before class started, and the paraprofessional or teacher read it to him so he knew what his choices were ahead of time. This support provided a visual to help him make good choices (alternative, "do instead" skills) when angry or bored. Another consequence map was used to teach him what would happen if he made inappropriate choices when angry or bored, as illustrated in "My Good Choices."

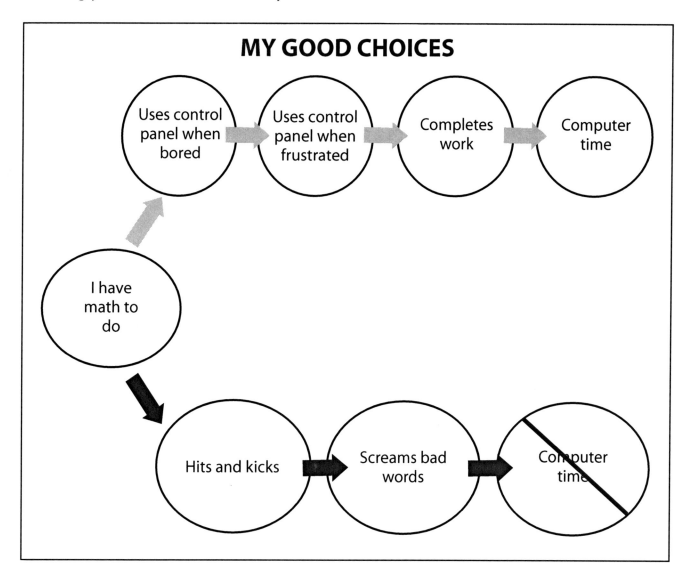

Will's map used a high-interest reinforcer and visually reminded him of his "green light" choices. The use of reinforcers or special interest activities has long been shown to increase positive behaviors (e.g., Heflin & Alaimo, 2007; Michael, 2004). The arrow was attached using a brad in the center of each "control" button and could be moved to the area (zone) that allowed him to "choose" what he wanted to do when these feelings came up. The "feel good" zone was when he was feeling good in class. When feelings of boredom or anger arose, he could move the arrow to an alternative and appropriate choice to deal with those feelings, thereby minimizing the amount of language he had to come up with. That is, by simply moving the arrow to "doodle on a piece of paper," he signified to the paraprofessional or teacher that he needed paper.

Even high-functioning children who appear quite verbal sometimes have a hard time communicating effectively during stressful situations. Using a support like this helps alleviate that problem while at the same time reducing disruption in the classroom that occurs when the teacher or paraprofessional needs to continuously give verbal and physical redirection.

Chapter 4: Language Mapping

Another type of mapping that is effective with students with ASD and related disabilities is Language Mapping. Instead of mapping out choices for what the student should be doing in response to instructions or feelings of frustration, Language Mapping provides choices to expand language. As such, this strategy is most appropriate for a student who has some language but lacks the skills to expand on and explain why she acts in certain ways or to use language effectively to communicate wants and needs, especially during stressful times, such as when suffering from sensory overload or facing a difficult math assignment.

Many students with ASD are able to communicate basic wants and needs, such as "I'm tired" or "I'm mad." But these phrases, although effective in many situations, lack the complexity needed for true social interaction. Thus, effective social interaction requires the ability to talk about why things are happening and what a person needs to be successful or enjoy the interaction and friendship more deeply.

Language Mapping goes beyond the "basics," giving choices to expand language so the student can indicate why he or she is feeling a certain way and request alternatives to deal with those feelings.

"When I Feel Mad" is an example of a language map used with Charlie, who was capable of saying, "I'm mad" when something did not go his way, but was not able to go beyond that and often became aggressive as a result.

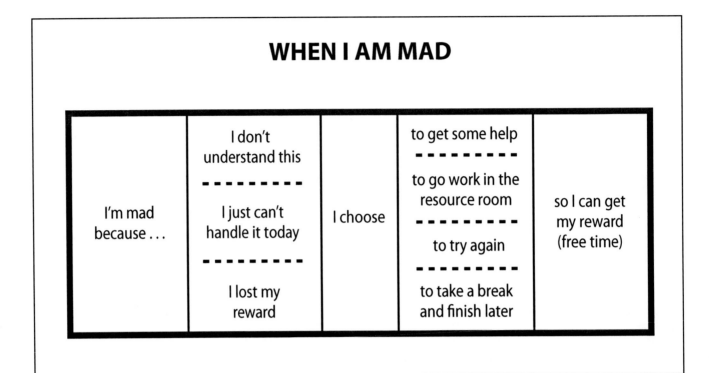

WHEN I AM MAD

| I'm mad because . . . | I don't understand this
- - - - - - -
I just can't handle it today
- - - - - - -
I lost my reward | I choose | to get some help
- - - - - - -
to go work in the resource room
- - - - - - -
to try again
- - - - - - -
to take a break and finish later | so I can get my reward (free time) |

We introduced the Language Map by placing it in front of Charlie when he was upset and reading it to him to increase his language skills. Because Charlie's aggressive behaviors were very severe and often hurt people, we also systematically worked on reducing aggressive behaviors using a strategy that reinforced Charlie when he refrained from any aggression, such as hitting or scratching. This strategy, known as a type of differential reinforcement (Cooper, Heron, & Heward, 2007), reduces aggressive behavior using reinforcement after an interval of time when behavior is not emitted. In other words, if the target behavior is screaming, the child might get to spend a few minutes with a favorite toy for every 5 minutes that she does not scream.

Charlie was prompted to point to the choices in each column of his map, "When I Am Mad," to formulate a sentence that would help him make a choice when he was upset, such as getting help, taking a break, or trying again. In the beginning, when we presented Charlie with the Language Map, we prompted him to formulate a sentence to communicate why he was mad. Often it was because his behavior required him to "try again" to get one of his reinforcers. When Charlie did not hit for 5 minutes, he got to watch a few minutes of a favorite movie. If he hit, we reset the timer and informed him that he had to go the entire 5 minutes without hitting to be allowed to watch the movie. This upset him, but not as much as just telling him with words only to "try again," which made him go into a full aggressive tantrum. We used the map to help him say, "I'm mad, **because** I lost my reward, **so I choose** to try again." This not only helped reduce his frustration but also taught him increasingly complex language. He was then able to stay calm enough to communicate his feelings so he could make a choice to "try again." When that happened, we started the timer over, and he was able to be successful.

Another of the options in the column on the map gives a choice of "why" Charlie was mad. The sentence, "I just can't handle it" is a choice when you are not sure why the child is feeling a certain way. For example, you might see that a child is mad because he is yelling and kicking. If she needs prompts to use a Language Map, it would be difficult to "help" her point to or say, "I'm mad because …" when you don't know the reason she is mad. Having the choice "I'm mad because I just can't handle it today so I choose …" allows you to prompt the child and help her make a choice of what to do about feeling mad without having to know why she is mad.

Charlie needed physical prompts (by pointing to choices for him) in the beginning, but he was able to use this map independently after about one week. Indeed, this Language Map, used with the behavior strategy that reinforced him after every 5 minutes without hitting, reduced his aggression from 54.2 aggressive incidents per day to 6.4 aggressions per day. Eventually, Charlie demonstrated one or two aggressive behaviors a week!

Language Maps can also be used for other areas where it is helpful for the child to tell you "why" he is feeling a certain way and what the choices are to "make it better." "Why" is a difficult concept to understand, and the Language Map can help facilitate the necessary language. For example, when a child is crying, it is helpful for her to have a visual to refer to so she can tell you why she is crying. In addition to expanding communication, maps can help teach students how to make choices that lead to reinforcers, or green light choices. Additional examples include Language Maps that indicate when the child needs to take a break, shown in the example "When I Am Frustrated," or is feeling sick, shown in the example "When I Don't Feel Good."

WHEN I FEEL FRUSTRATED

I'm frustrated because	I had a bad night at home - - - - - - - - I got in a fight with my friends	I choose	to go to the counselor - - - - - - - - - - to take a break and finish later	So I can concentrate better

WHEN I DON'T FEEL GOOD

I don't feel good today because . . .	I have a headache - - - - - - - - My stomach hurts - - - - - - - - I feel sick	I want	to take a break - - - - - - - - to lay my head down - - - - - - - - to go to the nurse	so I can feel better

Chapter 5: Problem-Solving Maps

Many children with ASD, especially those who are high functioning, tend to be "black-and-white" thinkers (Collucci, 2011) and have significant difficultly handling frustration and "shifting" from what they think should happen to what is actually happening. In other words, they don't see the "in-between" or "gray" areas. This is another example of the "rigid thinking" mentioned in the Intro-duction. This failure to problem solve often leads to explosive behavior and meltdowns as the child gets frustrated.

An excellent resource is Kerry Mataya's and Penney Owen's book, *Successful Problem-Solving for High-Func-tioning Students With Autism Spectrum Disorders* (2013), in particular the visual support, the Problem-Solv-ing Chart. As illustrated below, the chart has a circle in the middle where the teacher and student deter-mine a "problem." Surrounding the middle circle stating the problem, are four more circles with options for what to do about the problem: (a) Seek Help From an Adult, (b) Talk It Out and Compromise, (c) Let It Go and Move On, or (d) Let It Bother You.

The Problem-Solving Maps presented here are an excellent way to expand this strategy when the choice made by the student is number 2, "Talk It Out and Compromise." The purpose of Problem-Solving Maps is to teach kids how to compromise or "meet in the middle" when solving problems. As such, a Prob-lem-Solving Map can help children to see the "gray" and learn to compromise and solve problems. Spe-cifically, it helps kids to see that each person – the teacher/parent and the child – has a "need/want" for something. For example, the teacher "needs/wants" the child to do the math assignment, whereas the child "needs/wants" to take a break because the noise level in the classroom is overwhelming him.

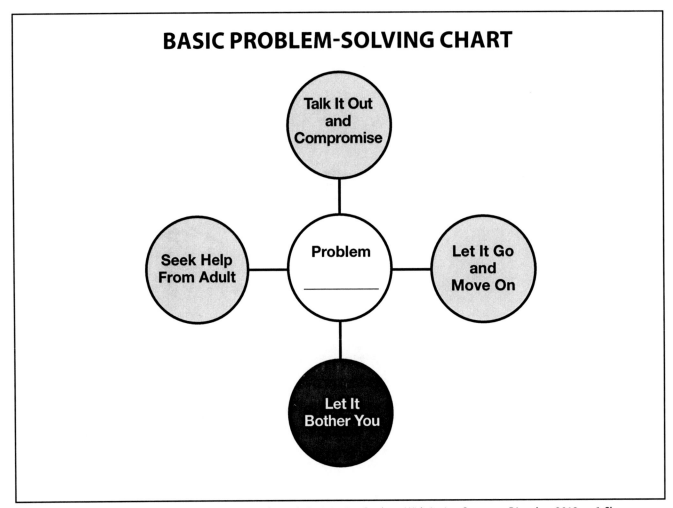

BASIC PROBLEM-SOLVING CHART

From K. Mataya & P. Owen, *Successful Problem-Solving for High-Functioning Students With Autism Spectrum Disorders*, 2013, p. 6. Shawnee Mission, KS: AAPC Publishing. Used with permission.

Problem-Solving Maps start with two rectangles, one on the left and one on right side, with a larger rectangle in the middle with lines for writing several options (see page 37). On the left side of the map, the teacher or parent, or the child, if capable, writes what the child needs or wants. On the right side of the map, the teacher or parent writes what he or she needs or wants. With the information specifically listed in the two rectangles, the child is often able to "see" there is a "problem," as visually depicted by listing the two "needs" on opposite sides of the paper in conflict with each other. That is, each person needs or wants something different.

In "Getting My Math Done," the child "needs" or "wants" to NOT do math (because it is hard and, therefore, frustrating), whereas the teacher "needs" or "wants" the child to practice math, show that she understands, and get a grade.

In the middle of the map is a larger rectangle, where solutions to the problem generated by both the child and the teacher/parent are listed. It is important that the child plays an active role in coming up

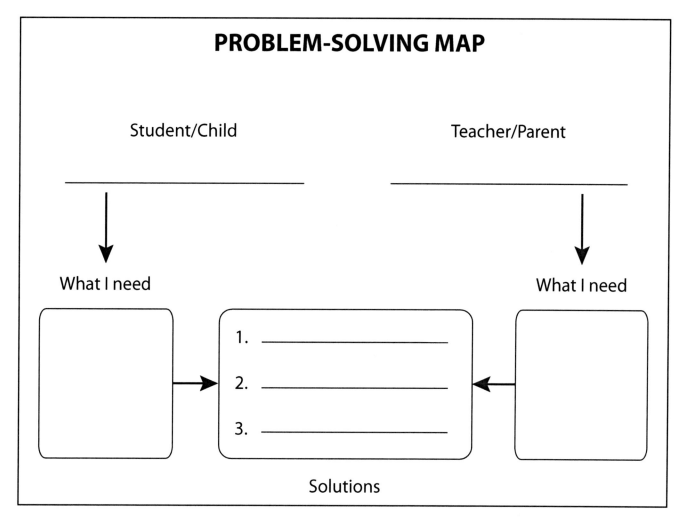

PROBLEM-SOLVING MAP

Student/Child   Teacher/Parent

_____   _____

↓   ↓

What I need   What I need

1. _____

2. _____

3. _____

Solutions

with possible solutions. Many kids can be taught that a compromise means "I get a little of what I want and you get a little of what you want!" This can be directly taught, for example, by using the example of two students who both want the one bag of candy left. The teacher can explain the meaning of compromise by dividing the candy in two and visually showing the "compromise."

In the beginning, children will need a lot of help and support. They may be "stuck" and unable to come up with any ideas or solutions. As a result, you will have to suggest some of the ideas and compromises. When listing the possible solutions in the middle of the map to the child, it important **not** to present them in an inflexible or authoritative way. For example, the choices should not be written by the teacher in this way:

1. Do the math

2. Lose recess

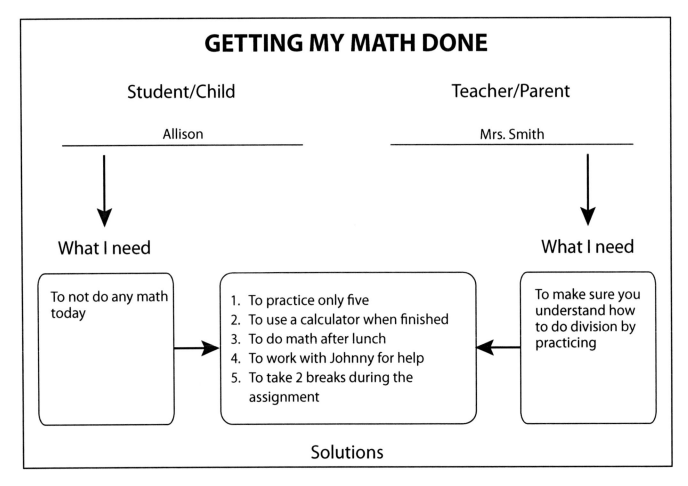

The map shows:

GETTING MY MATH DONE

Student/Child — Allison → What I need: To not do any math today

Teacher/Parent — Mrs. Smith → What I need: To make sure you understand how to do division by practicing

Solutions:
1. To practice only five
2. To use a calculator when finished
3. To do math after lunch
4. To work with Johnny for help
5. To take 2 breaks during the assignment

Instead, choices should be stated as ways to solve a problem, such as:

1. You do the first 5 math problems so I know you understand what I taught you, and then you can do the rest with the calculator.
2. You can do the math a little at a time and take two breaks during the time.
3. You can do just the even problems and also work with a partner.

The more you are able to present choices and ideas in this way, the more likely it is that children will eventually be able to come up with some of the solutions on their own.

"Honey on My Graham Cracker" and "Buying a Hunting Bow" are additional examples of how to develop and use Problem-Solving Maps. "Honey on My Graham Cracker" was used with my son Alex when he was 5. Alex often had explosive outbursts when things were frustrating and he was asked to "shift" his thinking or deal with a change. One evening, around 8:00 o'clock, I prepared a snack for him and his 3-year-old brother. I had just gone to the grocery store and purchased a box of Honey Maid Graham Crackers®. The box showed a drip of honey about to land on a graham cracker to suggest that the crackers were made of real honey. Alex, who was a very black-and-white thinker, wanted honey on his graham cracker like the box showed. Unfortunately, I did not have any honey.

Ideally, I would just have told him I did not have any and hope he would deal with it. However, I knew from the past that these kinds of things caused long, drawn-out meltdowns. To deal with the situation, we developed the map "Honey on My Graham Cracker." Alex could not read at the time, so I read it to him as we made the map together.

First, I wrote on the left side what Alex needed – honey on his crackers – and on the right what Mommy needed – for Alex to pick something else, something she already had on hand. Then I told him we had to "solve" this problem. I started giving him ways to "shift" and see other ideas. My first idea was to put peanut butter on the graham cracker, which he thought was the worst idea on the planet. He was still pretty upset. He was also too young, and at the time this strategy was too new for him to come up with ideas on his own. He was "stuck" with only wanting honey, so I had to help him by giving lots of ideas. It was important that I put it in a way that was not telling him he had to pick something else but in a way that "suggested" there were other ideas.

The second idea was to put chocolate sauce on the crackers. This suggestion was met with a curious "chocolate sauce???" accompanied by a look of raised eyebrows and a smile. When I reassured him that we could put chocolate sauce on his graham crackers, luckily, he thought this was a fabulous idea. In fact, it was better than honey.

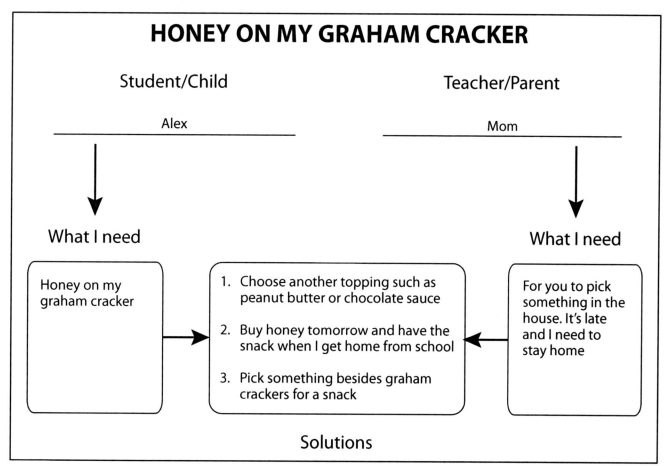

Alex's inability to "shift" and deal with the subsequent frustration prevented him initially from seeing any other options. If I had simply said, "No, I don't' have any honey," he most surely would have had another meltdown. However, on this night, the Problem-Solving Map meant a happy 5-year-old in bed by 8:30 – and a really happy mom.

The final example of a Problem-Solving Map, "Buying a Hunting Bow," reflects a time when my son was continuously asking to buy something. His tendencies toward obsessive-compulsive behavior caused him to ask for various things over and over. On this particular occasion, he was obsessing about getting a $285.00 compound bow, a type of bow used for deer hunting. We were able to solve the problem (Alex's constant begging to buy the bow) with the Problem-Solving Map shown below.

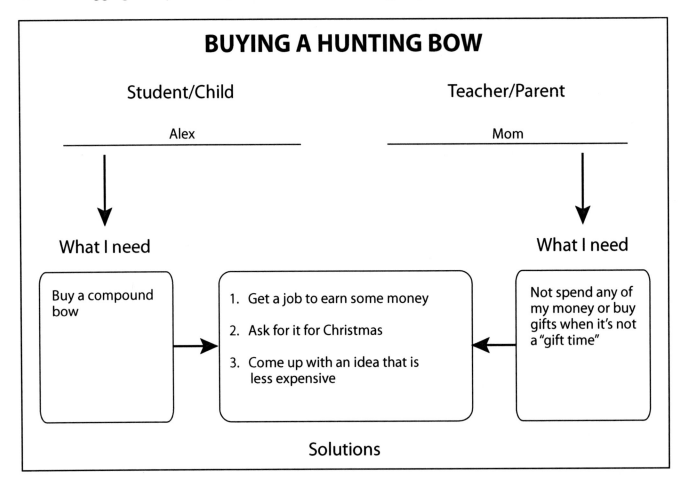

Chapter 6:
Behavior Maps in Action

By now, I hope you have realized that using Behavior Maps can be effective both within the classroom and at home. In this chapter, you will look at some additional examples of how to implement this strategy.

There are basically two ways to implement a Consequence Map. One is to introduce the map before a behavior occurs; the other is to use a map during the behavior. It is preferable to show the child the map before the behavior occurs so you can support her in making a positive choice and "prevent" the problem behavior from ever occurring. However, if the child is already upset, a Consequence Map can help tremendously by showing her a way to still make a good choice (cause) and get a reward (effect) for doing so.

Creating a Behavior Map Ahead of Time

By creating a behavior map **before** a behavior occurs, you help the child predict what the consequences will be for the behavior choices she makes, including the reinforcement she will receive upon demonstrating the appropriate behavior. The following example involved a student at our school.

Mike was a newly enrolled student in the sixth grade with autism and Down Syndrome. He also happened to weigh over 300 pounds. (The reason why his weight is significant will soon be apparent.) At the time, the program shared a playground with a school across the street because we did not have our own. The only stipulation to this arrangement was that our students could not be on the playground at the same time the other schools' students were there, due to our insurance.

On Mike's first day of school, we went to the playground at our designated time. Mike was very excited and immediately climbed to the top of the slide. Only once up there, he decided he was not going to come back down – EVER!! At 300 pounds, there was nothing I could do to physically get him down. After two hours, and in the meantime preventing 50 third graders from the other school from coming out for their recess, Mike finally came inside. Overall, Mike's first day at the Center was frustrating.

You may think to yourself, "Well, I'd solve that – just don't allow Mike to go to the playground any more!" But I didn't think that was fair to Mike. A consequence would not teach him anything useful for the future. Remember the all-important question is: "What do I want him to do instead?" In this case, I wanted Mike to walk appropriately back to school when recess was over.

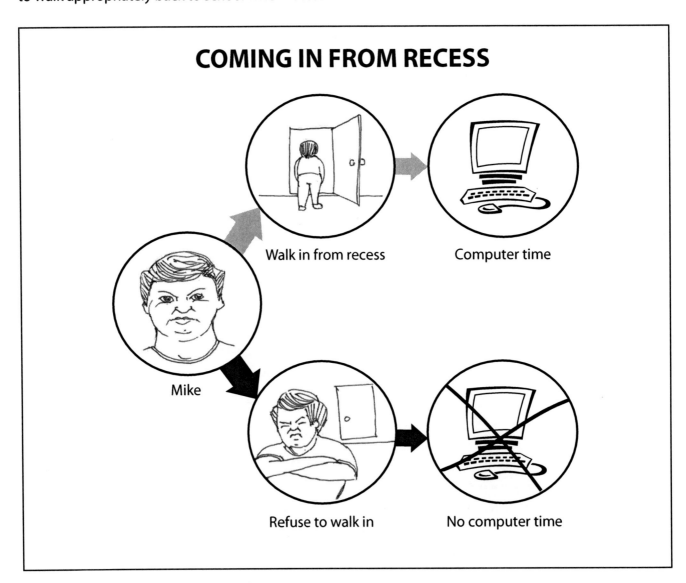

COMING IN FROM RECESS

Mike

Walk in from recess

Computer time

Refuse to walk in

No computer time

I started by determining how to reinforce the alternative behavior – the answer to the question: "What do I want him to do instead?" If you come in from recess, you usually have to do work, and that is not typically very reinforcing of appropriate behavior. To identify an effective reinforcer, I asked his mom about his favorite toys and other preferences. For Mike, it was time on the computer.

I then decided that if he did the right thing, which was walking to the building appropriately after recess, he could have 10 minutes of computer time. After I selected a reinforcer, I developed a Consequence Map to help Mike see how doing the right thing (coming in from recess) would result in 10 minutes of computer time.

Now I had everything in place – the Consequence Map and the computer time. "Coming in From Recess" helped Mike see how he could get computer time. We went over it every day for about a week right before recess. It worked great, and Mike never had a problem with recess again!!

Using a Behavior Map After a Tantrum or Other Inappropriate Behavior Has Occurred

Another way to use a Behavior Map is to create one after a behavior or tantrum has occurred. In such cases, the map may help the child calm down and redirect her to the appropriate choices she needs to make, as illustrated in "Time to Go Home."

I was doing a consultation with a school, and at the end of the day all of the students left to go home. As I was sitting in the room talking to the teacher, some of the staff brought one of the students back into the classroom in a complete aggressive meltdown. He was out of control – screaming, crying, and hitting them.

We immediately wanted to know what was wrong and knew the best way to do this was to talk to staff about what happened, specifically right before the behavior started. It turned out that the student thought his mom was picking him up, but it turned out that his grandma came instead. As mentioned earlier, children with ASD do not do well with unpredicted change, and the team was unaware of the change in pickup arrangements for the student and, therefore, had not been able to prepare him for it.

For the next 15 minutes, the staff and teachers tried to calm him down and "talk him into" going with Grandma. They also tried to get a hold of his mom but were unable to reach her. Each time they tried to talk to the student, he became more aggressive.

After witnessing this for a while, I decided to try to help by writing a Consequence Map, "Time to Go Home." As you can see, it was nothing fancy. The important thing was that I sat down next to the student and started to draw as well as talk out loud with him about what would happen IF he went with Grandma, trying to include what good things that might entail, like a snack and playing with friends. Luckily, on his own, he came up with the idea that he could play with his cousins. I think when he visually saw me put an X over the snack and an X over playing with his cousins as a result of him making the choice not to go home with his grandma, he realized the importance of following the map, which included going with Grandma. Admittedly, he was still crying and upset, but he took the map I drew him with him and decided to go with Grandma.

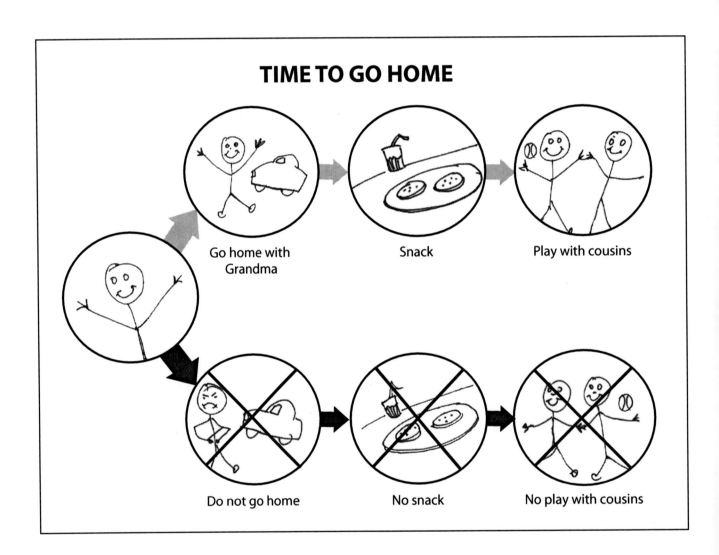

Conclusion

There is no limit to the number of ways you can use a Behavior Map. Behavior Maps can be used in all types of situations – when kids are feeling frustrated or when they use behavior to avoid requests from teachers and parents – and with a wide range of students, including those who can read and non-readers who need pictures.

Mapping is a visual strategy that is unique for every student. There isn't a perfect map that you can take from this book, copy, and use. To be effective, each map must be individualized to meet the unique needs of each student. With practice, you will become good at tailoring maps to the children you work with. I have used them for more than 15 years with great success.

I still find new ways to make and use maps all the time. For example, we are currently working with a way to use a Behavior Map to teach social skills to a child who is rude to his friends. Our intention is to show him with a Consequence Map the outcomes of yelling mean things at his friends and also write out specifically what "nice words" are so he has a visual prompt to remind him what to do.

I wish you great success using Behavior Maps with children who have ASD or any other developmental disability. They can significantly improve behavior problems and help each one of your students or children to be successful during school and at home.

References

American Psychiatric Association. (2013). *The diagnostic and statistical manual of mental disorders (V)*. Washington, DC: Author.

Brown, K. E., & Mirenda, P. (2006). Contingency mapping: Use of a novel visual support strategy as an adjunct to functional equivalence training. *Journal of Positive Behavior Interventions, 8,* 155-164.

Buron, K. D., & Curtis, M. (2012). *The incredible 5-point scale: The significantly improved and expanded second edition*. Shawnee Mission, KS: AAPC Publishing.

Collucci, A. Z. (2011). *Big picture thinking – Using central coherence theory to support social skills*. Shawnee Mission, KS: AAPC Publishing.

Cooper J. O., Heron, T. E., & Heward W. L. (2007). *Applied behavior analysis, second edition*. Upper Saddle River, NJ: Pearson Education, Inc.

Endow J. (2011). *Practical solutions for stabilizing students with classic autism to be ready to learn – Getting to go!* Shawnee Mission, KS: AAPC Publishing.

Gray, C. (1994). *Comic Strip Conversations™*. Arlington, TX: Future Horizons.

Gray, C. (2010). *The new Social Story™ book*. Arlington, TX: Future Horizons.

Heflin L. J., & Alaimo, D. F. (2007). *Students with autism spectrum disorders, effective instructional practices*. Upper Saddle River, NJ: Pearson Education, Inc.

MacDuff, G., Krantz, P., & McClannahan, L. (1993). Teaching children with autism to use pictographic activity schedules: Maintenance and generalization of complex response chains. *Journal of Applied Behavior Analysis, 26,* 89-97.

Mataya, K., & Owen, P. (2013). *Successful problem-solving for high-functioning students with autism spectrum disorders.* Shawnee Mission, KS: AAPC Publishing.

Michael, J. (2004). *Concepts and principles of behavior analysis* (rev. ed.). Kalamazoo, MI: Society for the Advancement of Behavior Analysis.

Myles, B. S., & Southwick, J. (2005). *Asperger Syndrome and difficult moments – Practical solutions for tantrums, rage, and meltdowns* (2nd ed.). Shawnee Mission, KS: AAPC Publishing.

O'Neill, R. E., Horner, R. H., Albin, R. W., Sprague, J. R., Storey, K., & Newton, J. S. (1997). *Functional assessment and program development for problem behavior: A practical handbook* (2nd ed.). Pacific Grove, CA: Brooks/Cole Publishing Company.

Otten, K. L., & Tuttle, J. L. (2011). *How to reach and teach children with challenging behavior – Practical ready-to-use interventions that work.* San Francisco, CA: Jossey-Bass.

Schopler, E., Mesibov, G. B., & Hearsey, K. (1995). Structured teaching in the TEACCH system. In E. Schopler & G. B. Mesibov (Eds.), *Learning and cognition in autism* (pp. 243-267). New York, NY: Plenum.

Tobin, C. E., & Simpson, R. (2012). Consequence maps: A novel behavior management tool for educators. *Teaching Exceptional Children, 44*(5), 68-75.

Volkmar, F. R., Klin, A., & Cohen, D. J. (1997). Diagnosis and classification of autism and related conditions: Consensus and issues. In D. Cohen & F. Volkmar (Eds.), *Handbook of autism and pervasive developmental disorders* (2nd ed., pp. 5-40). New York, NY: Wiley.

Winner, M. G. (2007). *Social Behavior Mapping® – Connecting behavior, emotions and consequences across the day.* San Jose, CA: Think Social Publishing, Inc.

Related Books From AAPC

Successful Problem-Solving for High-Functioning Students With Autism Spectrum Disorders

by Kerry Mataya, MSEd, and Penney Owens, MEd, BCBA; foreword by Brenda Smith Myles, PhD

Many individuals with autism spectrum disorders have difficulty coming up with effective ways to solve problems. *Successful Problem-Solving for High-Functioning Students With Autism Spectrum Disorders* teaches how to integrate the book's problem-solving chart into classrooms, homes and social skills groups to help individuals with ASD to learn to problem solve effectively. The book uses *The Incredible 5-Point Scale* as a resource to get individuals in the right frame of mind for tackling problem-solving.

ISBN 9781937473211 | Code 9082 | Price: $20.00

The Incredible 5-Point Scale:
The Significantly Improved and Expanded Second Edition; Assisting students in understanding social interactions and controlling their emotional responses

by Kari Dunn Buron and Mitzi Curtis

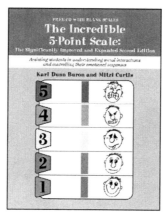

Using the same practical and user-friendly format as the first edition, Buron and Curtis let readers benefit from work done with the scales over the past 10 years, now considered "classics" in homes and classrooms across the country and abroad. Includes new scales specifically designed for young children and those with more classic presentations of autism, including expanded use of the Anxiety Curve. Another welcome addition is a list of goals and objectives related to incorporating scales in students' IEPs. Also, a free CD includes blank scales, small portable scales and worksheets for easy duplication. As in their other writings, the authors emphasize the importance self-management and self-regulation, two evidence-based practices.

ISBN 9781937473075 | Code 9936A | Price: $20.00
Also available as an ebook!

P.O. Box 23173
Shawnee Mission, Kansas 66283-0173
www.aapcpublishing.net

CPSIA information can be obtained at www.ICGtesting.com
Printed in the USA
LVOW09s0739150913

352254LV00002B/2/P